MEVLÂNÂ'S LIFE, WORKS

Dr. Erdoğan Erol

Anadolu Manşet Gazetesi, Culture Series, No: 8

ISBN: 975-00100-0-0

First published in   : 2005
Written and edited by : **Dr. Erdoğan Erol**
Translated by   : **M.Olcay Kabar**
Photographs by   : Özcan Tüfekçi
                            Zehra Önel
                            Cahit Sağlık
                            The archives of Altunarı Ofset

Layout/Graphics
Printing/Binding by : Altunarı Ofset Ltd. Şti.
 Kayalıpark PTT Arkası THK Pasajı Kat: 2 KONYA
Tel: 0090 332 353 69 69
http://www.mansetgazetesi.com
 e-mail: mansetgazetesi@ttnet.net.tr

THE LIFE OF MEVLÂNÂ

Muhammed Celâleddin, also known as Mevlânâ, Hüdâvendigâr, Rûmî, Sultân-ı Rûm, Ârif-i Rûm, Belhî, Farsguyî, Hünkâr, Pîr, Cenâb-ı Pîr Monlâ or Molla, was born on September 30, 1207 in Balkh, a city within the boundaries of current Afghanistan, but an important culture and art center of the Iranian Province Khorassan in the XIII. century, known as *Kubbetü'l İslam* (the Dome of Islam) and *Ümmül-Bilâd* (the Mother of Cities). (1)

Mevlânâ's father was Muhammed Bahaeddin Veled, the son of Hüseyin Hatibi, a prominent citizen of Balkh who was awarded the title Sultânü'l Ûlemâ (Sultan of the Scholars) during his lifetime. His mother was Mümine Hatun, the daughter of Rükneddin who was the Emir of Balkh. (2)

Sultânü'l Ûlemâ Bahaeddin Veled was forced to leave Balkh by certain political developments, the impending Mongolian invasion and the political and intellectual disagreement he had with Harzemshah.

According to the accounts of Eflâkî Ahmet Dede, **"In 1212 or 1213, they prepared three hundred camel-loads of valuable books, house-wares, food and the animals which would carry them. They departed from Balkh accompanied by fourty muftis, the family members and close friends."**(3) Mevlânâ was five years old while his brother

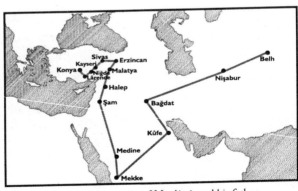

The migration route of Mevlânâ and his father
Muhammed Bahaeddin Veled from Balkh to Konya

4

Muhammed Alâeddin was seven at that time. (4)

Nishapur was the first stop of Sultânü'l Ûlemâ on the way, where they met Ferîdüddin Attar, the renowned theosopher. Mevlânâ was distinguished and appreciated by Ferîdüddin Attar at once despite his young age.

Ferîdüddin Attar said to Mevlânâ's father; **"this son of yours shall very soon set fire in the suffering hearts of this world"** and presented a copy of his work *Esrarnâme* (Book of Mysteries) to Mevlânâ. (5)

The caravan left Nishapur and set out first to Baghdad and then to Ka'aba through Kûfa. After performing the rites of pilgrimage, they went to Damascus on the way back. They met **Muhiddin İbnü'l Arabî** (1165-1240) there. İbnü'l Arabî, looking at young Mevlânâ walking after his father, said, **"There goes an ocean after a sea."**(6)

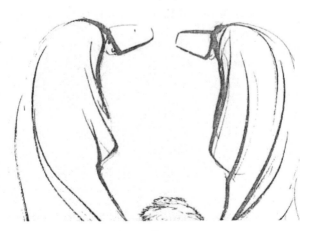

ما برای وصل کرده به آمدیم

نه برای فصل کرده به آمدیم

مولانا

I came here to unify
Not to divide.

Mevlânâ

Arrival of Sultânü'l Ûlemâ and his family at Lârende:

Sultânü'l Ûlemâ and his family went to Anatolia after Damascus and Aleppo and finally reached Larende (Karaman) in 1222 after passing through Malatya, Erzincan, Sivas, Kayseri and Niğde.

Emir Musa Bey, an honest and faithful Turk, was the governor of Karaman at that time. He ordered a medresse (theological school) to be built at the city center for Sultânü'l Ûlemâ and his household to settle (7) where they stayed for 7 years. **In 1225, at the age of 18, Mevlânâ married Gevher Hatun who was the daughter of Şerefeddin Lala, an esteemed personality in Karaman.** (8) **Mevlânâ had two sons from this marriage named Sultan Veled and Alâeddin Çelebi. Years later, after Gevher Hatun died, he married for the second time with Kerrâ Hatun who was a widow and already had a child. From this marriage, he had his son Muzaffereddin Emir Âlim Çelebi and his daughter Melike Hatun.** (9) He also had a step-son named Shemseddin Yahya who died at a young age.

The graves of 21 of the descendants of Mevlânâ, including his mother Mümine Hatun and his brother Muhammed Alâeddin, are still in the Aktekke Mosque in Karaman.

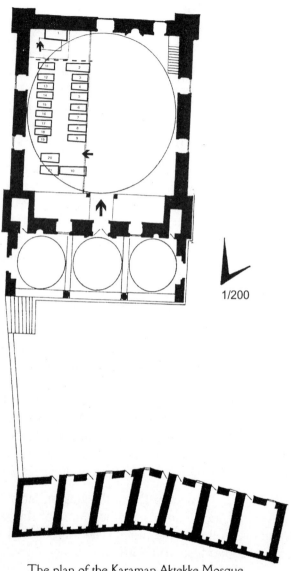

1/200

The plan of the Karaman Aktekke Mosque

A view of the Karaman Aktekke Mosque

Graves in the Aktekke Mosque:

1- **Mümine Hatun** (next to the wall of the mihrap, surrounded by wooden grating)
2- Karamanoğlu Emir Seyfettin Süleyman Bey - died in 1364
3- Ali Çelebi
4- Sheikh Ebu Bekir
5- Muhammed Çelebi
6- Ahmet Çelebi
7- Sheikh Veled Çelebi
8- Mustafa Çelebi
9- Ali Çelebi
10- **Muhammed Alâeddin Çelebi** - died in 1220 (Mevlânâ's elder brother)
11- 19- Mothers and other relatives from the Çelebi family (9 belongs to a child)
20- Muhammed Alâeddin
21- Abdurrahman Çelebi

Yâ Hazret-i Celâleddîn-i Rumî
Kudumunla müþerref eyledin Rumý

Oh blessed Celâleddîn-i Rûmî
You honored Anatolia with your presence.

This inscription is on the west column carrying
the entrance arch to the Semâhâne.

Migration of Sultânü'l Ûlemâ and His Family from Karaman to Konya:

A great part of Anatolia was under the reign of the Seljuks in the XIII. century with Konya as the capital. The city was noted with the abundance of art works, artists and scholars it embodied. The Seljuk Empire was enjoying its most prosperous days under the rule of Alâeddin Keykubâd who sent an invitation to Sultânü'l Ûlemâ Bahaeddin Veled and asked him to settle in Konya. (10)

Bahaeddin Veled accepted his invitation, left Karaman and came to Konya.

"All writers and scholars, together with the people of Konya, went to the entrance of the city to welcome Sultânü'l

10

Ûlemâ, as soon as it was heard that he was coming. Sultan Alâeddin dismounted from his horse at a distance. He went and kissed Sultânü'l Ûlemâ's knee as a sign of his respect. He waited for Baha Veled to shake hands with him but Baha Veled held out his sceptre instead of his hand."(11)

Alâeddin Keykubâd's intention was to welcome Sultânü'l Ûlemâ to his palace. But instead, Baha Veled went to the Altunapa (İplikçi) Medresse with his family and friends on March 3, 1228, saying, **"Medresse is for imams whereas *hânigâh* is for sheikhs, palace is for emirs, inn is for merchants, *zaviye* is for those who are vagabond and caravanserai is for those who are destitute."** It is said that this medresse was the only one in Konya at that time. (12)

Death of Sultânü'l Ûlemâ Bahaeddin Veled:

Sultânü'l Ûlemâ Bahaeddin Veled died in Konya on January 12, 1231 at the age of 85. (13)

His words **"The graves of mine, my children and their descendant's shall be here."**(14) were accepted as a testament and he was buried in the Rose Garden of the Seljuk Sultans at the spot where his grave still stands today in the Mevlevî Convent which serves as a museum since 1926. Later a Khorassan-plaster tomb was built over his grave with a marble inscription on it. **His tomb, becoming a sanctuary from the very first day it was built, was the first building of the convent which became a *külliye* (complex) later in time.**

Muineddin Pervâne, a follower of Sultânü'l Ûlemâ told Mevlânâ that he wanted to have an outstanding dome and arch constructed over his father's grave and asked his permission for this.

Mevlânâ refused this request saying, **"No domes you can build could be better than the sky itself. Then let the sky dome embrace his grave."**(15)   Upon Sultânü'l

Ûlemâ's death, his students and disciples started to gather around Mevlânâ. They regarded him as the only successor of his father and wanted him to take over his post. Mevlânâ, during his long education, achieved distinction as a scholar with considerable knowledge of religious sciences such as *tefsir* (interpretation), *hadis* (tradition) and *fıkıh* (canonical jurisprudence). He was giving sermons at the İplikçi Medresse which were attracting large crowds, but his spiritual training was not completed yet.

The interpretation of the Arabic inscription engraved on Sultânü'l Ûlemâ's marble tombstone is as follows:

"Only God is eternal. This is the grave of our *Mevlânâ* (our lord) and our master. The leader of the Muhammedan Tradition, source of wisdom, reviver of the tradition, destroyer of those who go astray from the Islamic rules, guide for the world and follower of the divine path, Sultan of the learned, *Mufti* (religios magistrate) of the east and the west, *Baha* (of great value) of the nation and religion, Sheykh of Islam and the Muslims, Muhammed b. al-Huseyin b. Ahmed al-Balkhi. May God be pleased with him and his ancestors. He passed away in the morning of Friday 18th of Rabiulakhir 628 H. (12 Jan. 1230)."(16)

13

Mevlânâ's Meeting Shems-i Tebrizi:

Shems-i Tebrizi, who was the son of Ali, the son of an Azerbaijani Turk called Melik-dâd, was also known as *Sultânü'l Fukarâ* (sultan of the poor), *Sultânü'l Gurebâ* (sultan of the destitute), *Sultânü'l Maşukîn* (sultan of the lovers) and *Shems-i Perende* (flying Shems) and was a disciple of *Selle-baf* (basket weaver) Sheikh Ebu Bekir. However, he attained to such a level of spiritual maturity one day that he could not be contented with his sheikh any more. So he set out on a journey in search of a greater sheikh. He decided to turn his way towards Anatolia when Rükneddin Sincabî said, **"You must go to Anatolia. Someone there is burning with love. You will go and enjoin him."**

It was November 15, 1244 when Shems-i Tebrizi, whose full name was Shemseddin Mehmed, the son of Ali, the son of Melik-dâd, encountered Mevlânâ. The meeting of the two at this place referred to as Merce'l Bahreyn (convergence of the two seas) was a turning-point in Mevlânâ's life. Eflâki Ahmet Dede describes the meeting of Mevlânâ and Shems in his work Menâkıbü'l Ârifîn as follows: (17)

One day, Mevlânâ and a group of scholars were passing by the *Pembe-Furuşân* (cotton sellers) Medresse after leaving the *Şeker-Rîzân* (candy makers) Inn. Having seen this, Shems got to his feet, took hold of his mule's reins and asked him: **"Tell me, the master of worldly and spiritual scholars and the savant of God's names! Who is greater? Muhammed or Bayezid?"**

Mevlânâ answered, **"Of course Muhammed Mustafa is the master of all prophets and holy people. He is the one who is greater."**

Picture depicting the meeting of Shems-i Tebrizi and Mevlânâ (painted by Ziya Ceran)

15

This time Shems-i Tebrizi asked: **"But Muhammed said, 'God I glorify you. I could not worship you the way you deserve.' while Bayezid said, 'I glorify myself. My reputation is so great. I am the sultan of sultans.'** "What would you say about this?"

Mevlânâ was startled at this question. He got down from his mule and answered Shems: **"Only one drop was enough to cease Bayezid's thirst. He wanted no more water. But Muhammed was burning from thirst and was never satisfied with one drop. Bayezid thought he was enlightened at the very first stage he arrived and got no further. Muhammed, however, was progressing everyday in the way of realizing the power and greatness of God. That is why he said, 'I could not worship you the way you deserve.'"**

Mevlânâ, who never pleaded or implored for anything from anyone by that time, went into seclusion with Shems who was at the age of sixty when they met. He closed his doors to everyone. He gave up his lectures and sermons. (18) He started to perform *semâ* (mystic whirling dance). He changed the way he dressed up. He became a student again. Shems was the match which set Mevlânâ on fire.

Mevlânâ's withdrawal from his students and disciples after the arrival of Shems in Konya led to the development of hostility towards Shems. This situation had become so distressing that the day came when Shems had to flee from Konya. He went to Damascus several times, but Mevlânâ managed to bring him back each time. Once, Mevlânâ sent his son Sultan Veled to Damascus to fetch Shems. (19)

Mevlânâ found "the existence of absolute maturity" in Shems' spirit and saw "the divine lights of God" in his face. Their companionship did not last long however. **Shems-i Tebrizi disappeared suddenly on the night of December 5, 1247.** (20) News spread around in Konya about his being murdered.

Various rumours were going around about his disappearance. It was said that he was murdered and thrown into a well by a group of people among which there was also Alâeddin, the middle son of Mevlânâ. It was also rumoured that Shems went away with his head cut off, carrying it under his arm or he simply flew away. Thus, several memorial tombs exist all attributed to Shems, two of which are situated in Konya and the others in Niğde, the Iranian cities of Tebriz and Hoy, and the city of Multon in Pakistan respectively. **However, it was found out by Mehmet Önder as a result of the research he** made at the place known as the memorial of Shems in the Mevlânâ Museum when he was the director that it was the actual burial place of Shems.

Mehmet Önder explains this incident as follows on page 101 of his book **"Mevlânâ and the Whirling Dervishes"**, under the title "A Memory": (21)

A miniature depicting Shems-i Tebrizî when he is about to be stabbed to death
(Sevâkıb-ı Menâkıb, XVII. century)

18

"One day, during my time as Director of Konya Mevlânâ Museum, I was busy with some research in the 'memorial' of Hz. Shems of Tabriz. While I was working, a trapdoor in the wooden base upon which the wooden sarcophagus rested caught my eye. When we lifted the trapdoor we saw that steps led down to a cellar underneath the tomb. After carefully cleaning the rubble and soil which blocked the steps we saw that just under the wooden sarcophagus in the room above, was a cellar cut out of stone, typical of Seljuk period tombs. And in one corner was a grave covered with Khorassan plaster.

When I saw this grave I was filled with excitement. This memorial might in fact be the real burial place of Shems. I wrote a letter to the scholar Abdulbâki Gölpınarlı informing him of what we had found and a few days later he arrived. Together we made our way down into the cellar. After investigating the room and the grave Gölpınarlı came to the firm conclusion that this was the grave of Shems himself. As a matter of fact, he mentioned this in the second print of his book 'Mevlânâ Celâleddin' letting me enjoy his compliments."

Selâhaddin Zerkûbî:

Mevlânâ lived in seclusion for many years after the death of Shems. He turned his face to Selâhaddin Zerkûbî with all his heart when he gave up hope to meet Shems again. He made his companions and followers obey him and appointed Selâhaddin as his successor for their enlightenment.

Selâhaddin was an illiterate gold-beater *(Zerkûbî)*. Mevlânâ's meeting Selâhaddin in front of his shop was as follows: (22)

One day, as he was passing by Sheikh Selâhaddin Zerkûbî's shop, Mevlânâ heard the rhytmic sound of the hammers of the gold-beaters and started to perform *semâ.* **A big crowd gathered around. Sheikh Selâhaddin Zerkûbî was informed that Mevlânâ was dancing. The Sheikh told his apprentices not to stop hammering even if the gold was damaged.** *Semâ* **lasted from the forenoon till the afternoon. After a while, Mevlânâ told them to stop.**

The sheikh entered his shop and saw that the shop was full of gold leaves. His

anvil and all the other equipment had turned into gold. He went out crying aloud and ordered the people around to loot his shop. He left working from then on and became precious as a ring stone. He became worldwide celebrated with this grace. It is said that his apprentices had hidden that golden anvil and later sold it. They spent the money they got for *semâ* practices and granted it to beloved friends.

Selâhaddin was a silent, gentle, generous, pious and mature man. Mevlânâ was so favourable to Selâhaddin that he had his son Sultan Veled marry Selâhaddin's daughter Fatma Hatun, to reinforce the relationship between the two families.

He taught Fatma Hatun to read the Kur'an and to write. Mevlânâ comforted Fatma Hatun at times when she was offended by her husband Sultan Veled and advised his son to treat his wife well. The companionship of Mevlânâ and Sheikh Selâhaddin lasted only 10 years until Selâhaddin fell ill all of a sudden. He died in **January of 1259** after a long term of illness.

His grave is to the north of the tomb of Sultânü'l Ûlemâ. His tomb was made of Khorassan plaster and the following lines were inscribed in Arabic on his marble tomb stone: (23)

God is eternal. This is the place of our sheikh, the sun of the learned, the banner of divine inspiration and knowledge, the sultan of dervishes, who is perfect in deed and word and gives confidence and peace to searching hearts, the greatest light of God, master of judgment, the sea of God's mysteries, the interpreter of unknown symbols and unequalled mystery, the imam of devotion, the Bayezid of the century, the Cüneyd of his time, the devotee of justice and religion, Feridun the goldsmith, the son of Yağıbasan from Konya. May God bless his mysteries. He died on the first day of the month of Muharrem in the year six hundred and fifty seven.

Çelebi Hüsâmeddin:

Hüsâmeddin Hasan, son of Mehmed, son of Hasan from Urmiye was praised by Mevlânâ in the preface of the Mesnevî as the key to the treasures of love, the trustee of the treasures of the world, the Bayezid and the Cüneyd of the time. His family had migrated and settled in Konya where he was born in 1225.

Hüsâmeddin Hasan is commonly known as Çelebi or Ahitürkoğlu. Hüsâmeddin's grandfather was known as Ahitürk in his lifetime since he was from the city of the courageous.

Hüsâmeddin was deeply devoted to Mevlânâ. Because of this, Mevlânâ esteemed him more than all of his other followers and even his relatives. He left the administration of his works to Hüsâmeddin. Mevlânâ wouldn't even talk in congregations at which Çelebi was not present.The prefaces of the 4th, 5th and 6th volumes of the Mesnevî reflect how estimable a position Hüsâmeddin had beside Mevlânâ.

The companionship of Mevlânâ and Çelebi lasted 15 years. Çelebi worked also as Mevlânâ's secretary during this time. Mevlânâ was asked once, "Who would you appreciate as your caliph?" He answered, "Our Çelebi Hüsâmeddin, the Cüneyd of the time, is the caliph of God."(24)

Çelebi formed the principles of the Mevlevî sect, together with Mevlânâ's son Sultan Veled, after Mevlânâ. **He is the only one who took the post for 11 years and became the leader of the Mevlevî sect, although not a lineal descendant of the family.** After him, those who took the post were patrilineal descendants of Mevlânâ with very few exceptions.

A Khorassan-plaster tomb with a marble inscription was built over Çelebi Hüsâmeddin's grave after he died on October 25, 1284. The interpretation of the Arabic inscription is as follows: (25)

This is the tomb of the sheikh of the sheikhs, the sun of the learned, the imam of divine inspiration and knowledge, the key of heavenly treasures and the trustee of worldly treasures, the Cüneyd and the Bayezid of his time, the glory of God, virtuous Hüsâmeddin Hasan, the son of Muhammed, known as Ahitürk, who was

the son of Hasan. May God bless all of them. He is from Urmiye. He is the follower of the Sheikh who said that he slept as Kurd and woke up as Arab. May God bless his soul. He died on Wednesday, the twelfth day of the month of şaban in the year six hundred and eighty three.

Mevlânâ's Death:

Mevlânâ, the prominent figure of the spiritual world fell ill and was suddenly laid up. It was no use although physicians worked very hard to cure him. Mevlânâ, being aware that he was dying, made the following will: (26)

I bequeath that you fear God, openly and secretly,

eat little,

sleep little,

talk little,

avoid all sins,

abide by fasting and prayer,

always stay away from lust,

bear the torment and the torture of people,

avoid being in close relationship with populace and decadents,

keep the company of men of maturity and knowledge.

Good people are those who are helpful to others.

And good words are those which are less but meaningful.

Thank only God.

Hail to those who believe in the oneness of God.

Eflâki expresses his feelings and thoughts about Mevlânâ's death as follows:

A mother would take care of a child better than an elder child. The substance of men is earth and the wood of the coffin is the child of earth. Coffin is deemed as the brother of men. And the earth is the mother. Therefore, it is better to leave the dead in the arms of the affectionate mother. (27)

Do the people know what death is? Death is seeing God for godly men. Would they ever fear and refrain from seeing Him? (28)

Mevlânâ believed that the day of death was also the day of rebirth. When he died, he would reunite with God, the beloved. Death was migrating from one land to another. With this belief, Mevlânâ referred to the day of death as **Şeb-i Arûs**, meaning wedding day or nuptial night. He thought:

What is death on this side is birth on the other side.

He willed his friends not to lament after him. On a wedding day, playing reed flute *(ney)*, tambourine *(tef)*, double-drum

27

(kudüm) and performing *semâ* should take the place of grief.

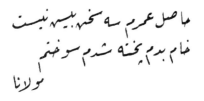

Mevlânâ, who summarized his life with the words "I was raw, cooked and burned."

died on Sunday, December 17, 1273 at sunset. Sadreddin Konevi would lead Mevlânâ's funeral service upon his will but he was so much grieved for losing his beloved Mevlânâ that he fainted. Subsequently the funeral service was led by Kadı Sıraceddin. (29) The next morning at sunrise, they took his coffin from the medresse and set off. Christians and Jews, Arabs and Turks, people from all religions and nations, pious scholars and rulers were present at his funeral. All went in front of the funeral holding their own holy books as entailed by their traditions. They were crying and reciting verses from the book of Psalms, the Old and New Testaments. They said, **"We understood the truth of Moses, Christ and other prophets from his clear statements; and we saw in him the nature and behavior of the prophets we have read about in our books. Just as you Muslims regard him as**

the Muhammed of his time, we also acknowledge him as the Moses and Christ of his time. We are his servants and disciples just as you are and we are even a thousand times more obedient to him.

Mevlânâ is the sun of the truths shining over humanity and scattering the light of grace upon them. The whole world loves the sun. All houses are enlightened by his light." A Greek Monk said, "Mevlânâ is like bread. Everybody needs bread. Have you ever seen any hungry man running away from bread?"(30)

The coffin was broken apart six times on the way. Each time they constructed a new one. It was already night when they arrived at the graveyard where his tomb took place. (31)

Mevlânâ was buried by the side of his father Bahaeddin Veled's grave at the place where the present mausoleum is located after an impressive funeral ceremony held on December 17, 1273.

Do not look for my grave in
the ground when I am dead!
My grave will be in the hearts of
The learned.
Hz. Mevlânâ

Mevlânâ's advice to his son: (32)

Bahaeddin! If you want to be in heaven, be friends with
   everyone.
Do not have grudge in your heart against anyone!
Do not want too much and do not surpass anyone!
Be like ointment and candle, not like needle.
If you do not want to be harmed by others,
   do not talk bad,
   teach bad,
   and think bad!
You will always be in joy if you mention others with
   friendliness.
And that joy is the heaven itself.
You will always be in sorrow if you mention others with
   hostility.
And that sorrow is the hell itself.
When you talk about your friends,
   the garden in your heart will bloom and be filled with roses and
   sweet basils. When you talk about your enemies,
   your heart will be filled with thorns and snakes.

You will get bored and feel tattered.

All prophets and holy people have behaved this way,

and reflected their character.

People have been fascinated by their good nature,

and chose to become their followers.

Mevlânâ warning his son Sultan Veled to avoid all sins (Sevâkıb-ı Menâkıb, XVII. century)

THE GREEN DOME

Alâmeddin Kayser, one of the followers of Mevlânâ, went to Mevlânâ's son Sultan Veled and reminded him of Mevlânâ's will: **"Our disciples shall construct our tomb at a high location so that it can be seen from long distances.**

Whoever sees our tomb from a distance, and believes in our faithfulness will be blessed by God. God will meet all the needs and wishes of those who come to visit our tomb with absolute love, perfect honesty, absolute truth and knowledge. All their wishes, either worldly or religious will be accepted. (33) He said that he wanted to have a tomb constructed over Mevlânâ's grave and he allocated 30 000 dirhems for this. Sultan Veled did not object to this request. This idea was also supported by Gürcü Hatun, the daughter of Gıyaseddin Keyhüsrev and the wife of Müineddin Pervane. She provided a fund of 80 000 dirhems. She also allocated 50 000 dirhems from the property of Kayseri. (34) The construction of the tomb started under the supervision of **Architect Bedreddin of Tebriz.** (35)

The construction took approximately one year. The tomb, resting over four piers, was completed in 1274. **The interior was decorated with stucco reliefs and the tomb was called *Kubbe-i Hadra* (Green Dome or Green Tomb) due to its conical cap covered with turquoise tiles.**

The mausoleum was typical of Seljuk art. The staircase leading to the crypt where Mevlânâ and his son Sultan Veled are buried is on the north side of the mausoleum. Not much is known about the crypt and its door because the entrance to the crypt was walled up.

The mausoleum, erected on four stone piers is walled only on the south side. The wall, the piers, the arches and the star-vault roof of the mausoleum are decorated with red, green, blue and gold colored brushwork tracery on plaster. Geometrical patterns, plant motifs and calligraphies are used in decorations in which symmetry is widely used. The decorations were restored from time to time during the Seljuk period, the period of principalities, the Ottoman era and even the Republican era.(36)

The inscription about the latest decorations of the mausoleum is located on the southern wall. It says in the inscription:

"The decorations of the Green Dome were made by Mevlevî Abdurrahman, the son of Mehmet from Aleppo, during the reign of Sultan Bayezid, whose magnificence is confirmed by God."

Heaven is depicted as a theme by poplars, date-palms and pomegranate trees on both sides and top of the stucco window on the southern wall of the mausoleum, bearing all the characteristics of the time.

According to the History of Karamanoğlu written by Şikârî, the 16-lobed body and the cap were built during the reign of Karamanoğlu

The south wall of the Green Dome

Alaeddin Bey. The cylindrical body of the mausoleum has 16 vertical lobes over which the conical cap rests which is also decorated with sixteen lobes. The tiles of the Green Dome were made in Kütahya in 1963. *Âyete-I Kursî* **(a verse from the Kur'an) is inscribed in *sülüs* style around the upper rim of the body just below the cap.**

On top of the conical cap of the dome is a crescent which is gilded with 8 micron-thick gold. There is no inscription about the construction of the mausoleum.

The Green Dome

WOODEN SELJUK SARCOPHAGUS

Mevlânâ's sarcophagus, a masterpiece of wood-carving, is made of walnut-tree. It is 2.91 m long and 1.15 m wide, with 2.65 m height at the head side and 2.13 m height at the foot side. (37)

Death themes were especially inscribed on the sarcophagus. Relevant verses from the Kur'an, couplets from Dîvân-ı Kebîr and odes were chosen for this purpose.

Rumî motifs and geometrical patterns which can be seen very often in Seljuk art of wood-carving were used to decorate the sarcophagus. The inscriptions and motifs are in bands and panels.

The name of the artist who made the sarcophagus is inscribed on the panel at the foot side which at the same time serves as the lid. It says in the inscription that the sarcophagus was made by Abdülvâhid, the son of Selim.

This sarcophagus was removed and placed over the sarcophagus of Mevlânâ's father Sultânü'l Ûlemâ Bahaeddin Veled in 1565 when Süleyman the Magnificent had a new big marble sarcophagus made over the tombs of Mevlânâ and his son Sultan Veled. When viewed from the front side of the Green Dome, only the head facade of the sarcophagus which is 291 cm high is visible. This facade is quite high compared to Mevlânâ's sarcophagus giving the impression as if

Mevlânâ's father is standing. This originated the legend that Mevlânâ's father stood up as a sign of respect for his son's great knowledge when his funeral was brought to his tomb. (38)

The following ode about death from Dîvân-ı Kebîr was engraved on the sarcophagus:

1. On the day of my death, when you see my coffin going by on shoulders, don't think that I care about leaving this world.

2. Don't weep for me, don't say, "Alas!" The time to say "alas" is when you are deceived by the Devil.

3. Don't think of departure when you see my funeral. For me, this is the time for union and meeting.

4. Don't say farewell when you put me into the grave, because the grave is only a curtain for those gathering in Paradise.

5. You have seen the sunset, now watch the sunrise. Can setting cause any harm to the sun and the moon?

6. What seems as setting to you is rising indeed. The grave seems like a prison, but it is the liberation of the soul from prison.

7. Are there any seeds sown in the ground and didn't grow at all? So why do you have doubt about the human seed?

8. Are there any buckets sent into a well and didn't come out full? So why should Joseph of the soul lament because of the well?

9. When you close your mouth on this side open it on the other side, because your cries will be beyond place in the sky.

A wooden sarcophagus was made in 1274 when Mevlânâ died and was buried here. This wooden sarcophagus, a masterpiece of Seljuk art, was removed when Mevlânâ's son Sultan Veled died on November 11, 1312 and was buried beside his father. The reason was that it was not sufficient to cover two graves because it was made only for one. **In 1565, during the reign of Sultan Süleyman the Magnificent, a new sarcophagus was placed instead of it which was made of sky-blue marble, measuring 3.10 m x 3.80 m, with a height of 0.90 m.** To indicate that there were two graves under it, two small wooden sarcophagi were located over the marble sarcophagus.

The marble sarcophagus had no inscription. If any inscriptions had been put on the two-cambered sarcophagus, there would have to be three: first one about the date of Mevlânâ's death, second one about the date of Sultan Veled's death and the third one about the date of the construction of the marble sarcophagus. It is likely that no inscriptions were put on the sarcophagus considering that three inscriptions would be too much for one sarcophagus. This causes a lack of information about the exact date of construction of the sarcophagus. (39)

The marble sarcophagus made in 1565
during the reign of Süleyman the Magnificient

Pûþîde (sarcophagus cover) was made in 1896 during the reign of Sultan Abdülhamid II, for the sarcophagi of Mevlânâ and his son Sultan Veled.

Sultan Abdülhamid II had the imperial cypher of Sultan Abdülhamid III embroidered on the foot side of the cover.

The calligraphies on the cover belong to Hasan Sırrı. Verses from the Kur'an were embroidered on the cover together with rose and tulip motifs.

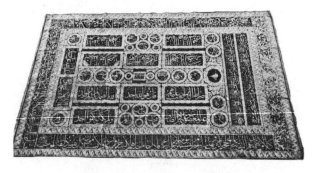

The sarcophagus cover made for the sarcophagi of Mevlânâ and his son Sultan Veled in 1896 during the reign of Sultan Abdülhamid II

من بنده قرآنم اگر جان دارم
من خاک ره محمد مختارم
گر نقل کند جز این کس از گفتارم
بیزارم از و و زین سخن بیزارم
مولانا

So long as I am alive, I am the slave of the Kur'an

I am the dust and the dirt on the path of Muhammed the chosen

If anyone misinterprets my words

I shall be complainant of both those words and of whoever misinterprets them

Mevlânâ (40)

43

MEVLÂNÂ'S NATIONALITY

Mevlânâ was born on September 30, 1207 in Balkh. Balkh is a city which lies within the boundaries of current Afghanistan. Since in many sources he is mentioned as **Mevlânâ Celaleddin of Balkh, he can be counted an Afghan citizen.** Balkh was a city of the Iranian Province Khorassan in the XIII. century. **Therefore, Mevlânâ can be counted an Iranian citizen as well.** But since Balkh is also associated with Afghanistan, Iranians called him **Mevlânâ Celaleddin-i Fars Guyî** (Mevlânâ Celaleddin who speaks Persian).

Turks, however, acknowledge him as a Turk, because his grave is in Konya where he spent more than 50 years of his lifetime; and call him **Mevlânâ Celâleddin Rumî** (Mevlânâ Celâleddin of Anatolia). Mevlânâ also expresses in one of his poems that he is Turk.

According to this, **Mevlânâ is Turk.**

Mevlânâ invited the humankind to friendship, brotherhood, love and solidarity with no discrimination on grounds of language, religion, race and complexion. Mevlânâ's philosophy and ideas attracted the attention of large numbers of people and thus became universal. This made Mevlânâ a world citizen, rather than an Afghan, an Iranian or a Turkish citizen.

How fortunate our world is to have a citizen like Mevlânâ.

بیگانه مگیرید مرا زین کویم

در کوی شما خانهٔ خود می جویم

دشمن نیم ار چند که دشمن رویم

اصلم ترکست اگر چه هندی گویم

مولانا

Don't treat me as a stranger, I am from this village.

I am looking for my house in your village.

I may look like an enemy yet I am not.

My origin is Turkish although I speak Hindu.

Mevlânâ (41)

WORKS OF MEVLÂNÂ

1- Mesnevî

2- Dîvân-ý Kebîr

3- Mecâlis-i Seb'a

4- Mektûbât

5- Fîhi Mâ Fîh

MESNEVÎ

Mesnevî is the name given to a certain style of poetry in classical eastern literature. In poems written in this style, the second hemistich of each couplet is in rhyme within itself. In other words, it has "a-a, b-b, c-c, d-d, e-e..." sort of rhyme order. The rhymes of a couplet do not have to be in harmony with neither the previous couplets nor the following ones. Mesnevî style was preferred for long themes and stories to be narrated in verse form because of its easy rhyme scheme.

Even though mesnevî is a style in classical eastern poetry, "Mesnevî of Mevlânâ" comes to mind with the word "mesnevî". (42)

Mevlânâ wrote the Mesnevî upon Çelebi Hüsameddin's request. One night, when they were alone, Çelebi, referring to the large number of Mevlânâ's poems written in gazel form, requested him to write a book similar to **the İlâhinâme of Senaî or Mantukuttayr of Attar.** Mevlânâ took a piece of paper from among the folds of his turban, on which the first 18 couplets of the Mesnevî were already written, with **"Listen to this Ney, while it's complaining,"** as the first line, and **"So cut a long story short and say to him Goodbye."** as the last. Mevlânâ then asked if Çelebi Hüsameddin would write down what he would dictate.

Çelebi Hüsameddin's writing down the Mesnevî for Mevlânâ is explained by Eflâki in Menakıbü'l Ârifîn as follows: **"Mevlânâ would recite the Mesnevî couplets when they were relaxing at Meram, when they were at hamam, during their walks and even when they were performing *semâ*. Çelebi Hüsameddin would write down quickly and then read them back to Mevlânâ. The writing of the Mesnevî was interrupted for two years with the death of Hüsameddin**

Picture representing Mevlânâ dictating the Mesnevî to Çelebi Hüsâmeddin (painted by Ziya Ceran)

48

Çelebi's wife. The second volume was started to be written again in 1264."(43)

The Mesnevî was written in Persian. **The oldest available copy of the Mesnevî which is dated to 1278 and is displayed at the Mevlânâ Museum consists of 25.618 couplets.** Later, the two most proficient names after Mevlânâ, Sultan Veled and his secretary Çelebi Hüsâmeddin gave a thorough reading to the manuscript of the Mesnevî. Misspellings were corrected by them and the omitted couplets were added on page sides with a special red ink named *surh*. This copy is also the one in best condition. (44)

Measure of the Mesnevî is:

Fâ i lâ tün - Fâ i lâ tün - Fâ i lün

Mevlânâ expresses his *Sufi* thoughts and philosophy in the 6 volumes of the Mesnevî as consecutive stories. He leaves the story he narrates and starts another one. He passes from one story to another and then turns back to the initial one and completes it.

It is possible to encounter signs of traditions *(hadis)* and verses from the Kur'an in every couplet of Mevlânâ's Mesnevî. As a matter of fact, some people believed that the Mesnevî was the narration of the Kur'an in the form of stories and named the Mesnevî as "Magz-ı Kur'an" (the essence of the Kur'an). We can say that the

Mesnevî is the book which was most interpreted after the Kur'an and *Hadis*.

Molla Camî, who said that the Mesnevî was the Holy Kur'an written in Persian, wrote the following quatrain:

Whoever reads the Mesnevî night and day,

> **Shall be far from hell,**
> **How shall I describe this noble man?**
> **He is not a prophet but has a book.**

The Mesnevî was widely read and interpreted in Mevlevî convents and mosques by *mesnevîhâns* (experts on interpretation and recitation of the Mesnevî) after Mevlânâ. Special schools under the name "Darü-l Mesnevî" were established where only the Mesnevî was taught.

The following is what Mevlânâ said about how widely the Mesnevî would spread and be read:

The Mesnevî will cover the whole world and seasons from the place where this spiritual sun rises to the place where it sets. There will be no circles or assemblies left where these words have not been read. It will even be read in places of worship and places of pleasure and enjoyment; all nations will be embellished with these words and benefit from them. (45)

51

The first eighteen couplets of the Mesnevî:

Listen to this Ney, while it's complaining,
The story of separation from God it's explaining.

> *Ever since they plucked me from my original ground,*
> *Men and women cry upon my painful sound.*

I need a breast pierced with the yearning of separation,
So that I may tell the meaning of my painful lamentation.

> *If anyone from his origin may ever fall away,*
> *He seeks a chance to find it in a better way.*

In every sort of company I cry, lament and moan,
Both the happy and the unhappy are charmed by my tone.

> *According to their opinions they have become my friend,*
> *Little do they bother to discern my esoteric trend.*

My secret is not concealed from my moaning cries,
But this light is not given to many ears and eyes.

> *The soul and the body aren't from each other concealed,*
> *But to many an ear and eye this factor is not revealed.*

This breath in the Ney is fire and isn't a sheer blow,
He who hasn't this fire let him die and let him go.

> *It is the fire of love that has made the Ney demented,*
> *And is love-desire that renders the wine fermented.*

The Ney is a friend to those who lose their companions,
Our breasts are also pierced like the Ney's divisions.

> *Who has ever seen an antidote and poison like the Ney?*
> *Who has ever seen a consoling friend like the Ney?*

The Ney is telling stories of the perilous ways and coils,
The love stories of Majnun and his bloody toils.

> *The knower of these feelings is none but a senseless one,*
> *Only an ear can be a customer of a speaking tongue.*

Our sorrows have made our days from us go astray,
While the days have followed time to make us their prey.

If the days are passing, worry not, let them pass away,
O Thee, the Only Pious One, with me prolong Thy stay.
If you aren't the fish with water you're soon tired,
If you haven't any daily bread, time is for you undesired.
For a lower man the stage of a perfect man is too high,
So cut a long story short and say to him "Goodbye."

Mevlânâ (46)

The first eighteen couplets of the
oldest copy of the Mesnevî dated 1278

DÎVÂN-I KEBÎR

Dîvân is the name given to the notebook in which poets collect their poems. Dîvân-ı Kebîr means "Big Notebook" or "Big Dîvân".

All of the poems written by Mevlânâ on various subjects are collected in this book. Although the language used in Dîvân-ı Kebîr is basically Persian, there are also some poems in Mevlânâ's Dîvân written in Arabic, Turkish and Greek. He used all these languages in their colloquial forms.

Dîvân-ı Kebîr consists of 21 small dîvâns (bahir) and another collection called the Rubai Dîvân. There are over 40 000 couplets in Dîvân-ı Kebîr.

Dîvân-ı Kebîr is also called **Dîvân-ı Shems** since Mevlânâ wrote some of his poems in this collection with the pseudonym Shems. The poems in the Dîvân are arranged according to their measures and rhymes.

Abdülbaki Gölpınarlı states the following about Mevlânâ's Dîvân-ı Kebîr in one of his works: **"Mevlânâ would easily be impressed by daily events and would start reciting his feelings while he was performing semâ in ecstasy and pour them into the mould of measure and rhyme. Those who gather around him would accept each word of him as inspiration. Among them, those who were called 'Kâtib-i Esrar' (writers of secrecy) and who entrust themselves noting down his poems would immediately write them down. Later, these** small collections *(bahir)* were put together in alphabetical order and 'Dîvân-ı Kebîr' was formed.

There is no difference between Mevlânâ's poems in the Dîvân and the Mesnevî considering literary style, expression and passion. In other words, the Dîvân and the Mesnevî are similar in style, expression, approach and substance. The only difference between these two works is form and measure.

In his poems, Mevlânâ made use of allegories and proverbs pretty often. Traditions, common beliefs, folk songs, even common swear-words are the basic elements of Mevlânâ's poetry. A continuous impression of freedom is felt in his poems. Every single poem is a whole. He worked on the same theme starting from the first couplet till the last without changing his course. He wrote as many couplets as he wanted. Some of his odes consisted of only four couplets while some others were much longer."(47)

The Seljuk binding of Dîvân-ı Kebîr with inventory number 69

On the interior side of the tuck of the binding of
Dîvân-ı Kebîr, it is written:

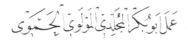

From this inscription we can understand that the name of the
bookbinder is **Mevlevî Ebubekr from Hama**. (48)

MECÂLIS-İ SEB'A

Mecâlis-i Seb'a (49), as indicated by the name itself, is the seven sermons of Mevlânâ, arranged as a collection of the notes written down by Mevlânâ's son Sultan Veled, Çelebi Hüsâmeddin and other followers of him who were present at his discourses.

Some additions were made later without changing the essence. The work was most probably corrected by Mevlânâ himself after it had been compiled.

Mevlânâ, who regarded poetry as a means of expressing his thoughts but not as an end by itself, commented on the following issues in his seven courts:

1. Ways of retrieval for societies which went astray.

2. Avoiding crime. Getting rid of heedlessness by reasoning.

3. The power of faith; sultan and humble servant.

4. Whoever repents and finds the right way becomes the beloved servant of God.

5. Value of knowledge. Ego and human groups.

6. Getting into heedlessness.

7. Importance of the mind. Knowledge and wisdom.

In these seven courts, 41 more traditions (hadis) were also given besides the main ones commented on. Each tradition chosen by Mevlânâ had a social context. Mevlânâ started each section by thanking and praising God and praying. He made his subjects and *Sufi* ideas more striking with stories and poems. The same style was also used in the Mesnevî.

Couplets from Sultan Veled's Mesnevî called İbtidâname can also be found in Mecâlis-i Seb'a. Besides, some stories from Makâlat of Shems were added into the first section.

MEKTUBAT (LETTERS) (50)

Mektubat is the collection of 147 letters written by Mevlânâ mainly to the Seljuk Sultans and the leading people of the time, either to give advice or to give enlightening information on religious and scientific issues for which his opinion was asked. Four of them are in Arabic while the remaining 143 are in Persian.

In his letters, Mevlânâ did not use a literary style, but instead wrote exactly as he talked. He never used such expressions as "your servant" in his letters.

Except titles of position and profession, he would use address words which suited best the wisdom, belief and accomplishments of the person he was writing to.

Mevlânâ was open, convincing and reasonable in his letters as he was also in his conversations. He started his letters with expressions like "God is the one who opens all doors". The language he used was conversational Persian.

His letters do not have dates on them. Thus it is not possible to put them in a chronological order. But from the historical incidents he referred to in some of his letters, we can estimate the approximate dates of those letters.

In his letters, Mevlânâ supports the main subject with examples. He refers to traditions (hadis), passages and verses from the Kur'an which suit the subject, gives quotations from the holy people and narrates explanatory tales. Mevlânâ's letters are totally associated with the way and the time he lived.

Some of his letters were just friendly letters. Some others, however, were written to transfer the complaints of unjustly treated people to relevant places and ask for compensation. All of the requests in his letters were granted.

FÎHI MÂ FÎH

Fîhi Mâ Fîh (51) means **"what he has in him is in him"**. It is one of the three prose works of Mevlânâ. It is the collection of Mevlânâ's conversations at various gatherings, put together by his son Sultan Veled. It is composed of 61 sections. Some of those sections were addressed to Süleyman Pervane, the Seljuk Visier, who was at the same time a close friend of Mevlânâ. This work is also regarded as a historical source because there are references in it to some political events.

The issues in this work are about heaven and hell, this world and the other world, master and disciple, love and *semâ*.

BIBLIOGRAPHY

1. Ahmet Eflâkî, Ariflerin Menkıbeleri (Çeviri, Tahsin Yazıcı), Şark İslâm Klasikleri, 29, M.Eğitim Basımevi, İstanbul 1989, c.I, s.77.
2. Eflâkî, c.I, s.8.
3. Eflâkî, c.I, s.9.
4. Eflâkî, c.I, s.12.
5. Devletşah, **Devletşah Tezkiresi** (Çeviren-Necati Lügal), 1001 Temel Eser, 112, İstanbul, 1977, s.249.
6. Mithat Baharî Beytur, **Divân-ı Kebîr'den Seçme Şiirler,** M.E. Basımevi, İstanbul 1965, s.XVIII.
7. Eflâkî, c.I, s.22.
8. Eflâkî, c.I, s.23.
9. Eflâkî, c.II, s.385.
10. Eflâkî, c.I, s.24.
11. Eflâkî, c.I, s.25.
12. Eflâkî, c.I, s.26.
13. Eflâkî, c.I, s.30.
14. Eflâkî, c.I, s.54.
15. Eflâkî, c.I, s.499.
16. Prof.Dr.Erkan Türkmen, The Essence of Rumi's Masnevi, Including His Life and Works, Eris Booksellers, Damla Ofset A.Ş., Konya, Turkey, 1997, p.13.
17. Eflâkî, c.I, s.91.
18. Eflâkî, c.I, s.92.
19. Eflâkî, c.II, s.65.
20. Eflâkî, c.I, s.93.
21. Mehmet Önder, Mevlânâ and the Whirling Dervishes, Güven Matbaası, Ankara, Turkey, 1977, p.101.
22. Eflâkî, c.I, s.464.
23. Abdülbakî Gölpınarlı, **Mevlânâ'dan Sonra Mevlevîlik,** s.357.
24. Eflâkî, c.II, s.8.
25. Abdülbakî Gölpınarlı, **Mevlânâ'dan Sonra Mevlevîlik,** s.360.
26. Eflâkî, c.II, s.7.
27. Eflâkî, c.I, s.190.
28. Eflâkî, c.I, s.297.
29. Eflâkî, c.I, s.390.
30. Eflâkî, c.II, s.13.
31. Eflâkî, c.II, s.14.

32. Eflâkî, c.II, s.213.
33. Eflâkî, c.I, s.440.
34. Emine Yeniterzi, **Mevlânâ Celâleddîn Rûmî,** T.Diyanet Vakfı Yayını No:161, Fotomekanik Ofset, Ankara 1995, s.16.
35. Eflâkî, c.I, s.151-420.
36. Hasan Özönder, **Mevlânâ Külliyesinin Tamir ve İlaveleri,** Selçuklu Dergisi, Sayı:2, S.Üniversitesi Matbaası Konya, 1988, s.13.
37. Mehmet Önder, **Mevlânâ Müzesi Şaheserlerinden Mevlânâ'nın Sandukası,** Ülkü Basımevi, Konya, 1958
38. Erdoğan Erol, **Mevlânâ Gelince Babası Ayağa Kalktı mı?,** Altunarı Ofset, Konya, 2002.
39. Erdoğan Erol, **Padişah III. Selim'in Mevlânâ'nın Türbesi için yaptırdığı Puşide,** Türk Etnoğrafya Dergisi, Sayı: XIX, Ankara Üniv. Basımevi, 1991, s.9.
40. Şefik Can, **Hz. Mevlânâ'nın Rubaileri,** Rubaî 1496.
41. Şefik Can, **Hz. Mevlânâ'nın Rubaileri,** T.C. Kültür Bakanlığı Yayınları, 2572, Kuban Matbacılık, Ankara 2001, Rubaî-1311.
42. Eflâkî, c.II, s.18.
43. Eflâkî, c.II, s.155
44. Abdülbakî Gölpınarlı, **Mesnevî ve Şerhi,** T.C. Kültür Bakanlığı, Özkan Matbaacılık, Ankara 2000.
45. Eflâkî, c.I, s.470.
46 Prof.Dr. Erkan Türkmen, A Bouquet of Rumi's Versified Poems, Misket Ltd., Konya, Turkey, 1996.
47. Abdülbakî Gölpınarlı, **Dîvân-ı Kebîr,** Kültür Bakanlığı Klasik, Sistem Ofset Matbaacılık, Ankara, 2000.
48. Erdoğan Erol, **Bir Selçuklu Cildi ve Mücellidi,** Hacettepe Üniv. Edeb.Fak.Sanat Tarihi Bölümü Prof. Dr. Aynur Durukan Armağanı. Rekmay Reklam, Ankara, 2002, s.235.
49. Abdülbakî Gölpınarlı, **Mecâlis-i Seb'a,** Kent Basımevi, İstanbul, 1994.
50. Abdülbakî Gölpınarlı, **Mevlânâ Celâleddin Mektuplar,** İnkılâp Kitabevi, İstanbul, 1999.
51. Abdülbakî Gölpınarlı, **Fîhi Mâ-fîh,** Altunarı Ofset Ltd. Şti, Konya, 2001.